discover countries

Discover Australia

Chris Ward

PowerKiDS
press.

New York

Published in 2012 by the Rosen Publishing Group, Inc.
29 East 21st Street, New York, NY 10010

First Edition

Concept Design: Jason Billin
Editors: Nicola Edwards and Jennifer Sanderson
Designer: Amy Sparks
Picture Research: Amy Sparks
Consultant: Elaine Jackson

Photographs:
Cover images, Shutterstock/Debra James; 1, Shutterstock/kaarsten; 3 (top), Shutterstock/Chee-Onn Leong; 3 (bottom) Shutterstock/urosr; 4 (map), Stefan Chabluk; 5, Shutterstock/Taras Vyshnya; 6 Shutterstock/Chee-Onn Leong; 7, Shutterstock/Abilsborough; 8, Paul A. Souders/Corbis; 9, Corbis/Will Burgess/Reuters; 10, Shutterstock/Dmitri Kamenetsky; 11, Shutterstock/Neale Cousland; 12, iStockPhoto/Gary Radler; 13, Shutterstock/urosr; 14, Shutterstock/Ximagination; 15, Shutterstock/Kaspars Grinvalds; 16, Shutterstock/Paul A. Souders; 17, LOOK Die Bildagentur der Fotografen GmbH/ Alamy; 18, Shutterstock/Chee-Onn Leong; 19, Corbis/Andrew Watson/JAI; 20, Shutterstock/fritz16; 21, Shutterstock/Ben Jeayes; 22, Shutterstock/deb22; 23, Corbis/Jon Hicks; 24, Shutterstock/BMCL ; 25, Shutterstock/Neale Cousland; 26, Shutterstock/Debra James; 27, Shutterstock/Dkrzowsk; 28, Shutterstock /kaarsten; 29, Shutterstock/Debra James.

Library of Congress Cataloging-in-Publication Data

Ward, Chris, 1973–
 Discover Australia / by Chris Ward. — 1st ed.
     p. cm. — (Discover countries)
 Includes index.
 ISBN 978-1-4488-6620-5 (library binding) — ISBN 978-1-4488-7046-2 (pbk.) —
ISBN 978-1-4488-7047-9 (6-pack)
1. Australia—Juvenile literature. I. Title.
 DU117.W29 2012
 994—dc23
                                2011028890

Manufactured in Malaysia

CPSIA Compliance Information: Batch #WW2102PK: For Further Information contact Rosen Publishing, New York, New York at 1-800-237-9932

Contents

Discovering Australia

Australia is an island in the South Pacific and is the world's sixth largest landmass. It is the only country in the world that is also a continent.

New Beginnings

Australia's first people are believed to have come from Asia around 40,000 to 65,000 years ago. These Indigenous Australians included the Torres Strait Islanders and the Aboriginal people, both of whom still live in Australia. In 1770, the British explorer James Cook arrived in the country and claimed it for Great Britain. Soon, thousands of British and Irish people were living in Australia. They were followed by Italians, Greeks, other Europeans, and, more recently, by people from Asia and the Middle East.

Australia Statistics

Area: 2,988,902 sq. miles (7,741,220 sq. km)

Capital City: Canberra

Government Type: Federal parliamentary democracy

Bordering Countries: None

Currency: Australian dollar

Language: English 78.5%, Chinese 2.5%, Italian 1.6%, Greek 1.3%, Arabic 1.2%, Vietnamese 1%, other 8.2%, unspecified 5.7%

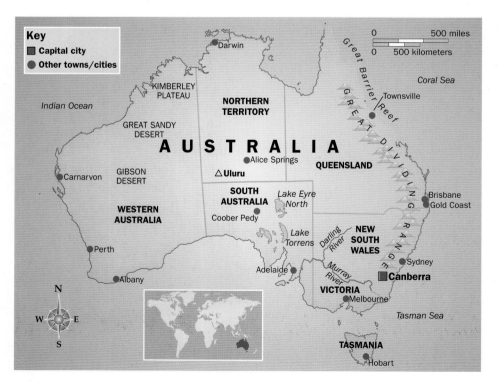

Australia is 32 times the size of the UK and more than 11 times bigger than the state of Texas.

This is the dramatic view across Sydney's harbor, the area in which Australia's first European settlers arrived.

An Independent Country

Australia became independent from Great Britain in 1901, but still has close ties. The British monarch remains the head of state and Australia is a member of the Commonwealth of Nations, an organization of countries that were mostly governed by Great Britain. Australia is now a powerful country in its own right. It has strong trade links with its Asian neighbors and plays an important role in world affairs. For example, Australian forces have been involved in the global fight against terrorism.

Unique and Challenging

Australia has many unique features, from its Aboriginal culture to its unusual wildlife and plants. These have developed in part because Australia was so isolated from other parts of the world. Today, this isolation presents challenges, too. Climate change is having a big impact on Australia and its growing population is putting great pressure on resources such as water (see page 7). One of the country's responses to climate change has been to create some of the most water-efficient farming systems in the world.

DID YOU KNOW?
Australia has some of the world's deadliest animals including the inland taipan, or fierce snake. This is the most venomous land snake in the world.

Landscape and Climate

The Red Center, or Outback, dominates the Australian landscape. It is a vast area of hot, dry rock and sand, which includes the Great Victoria, Great Sandy, Simpson, and Gibson deserts. Australia's other main feature is its coasts. Most people live and work along the coasts.

Mountains

Most of Australia is fairly flat. A chain of low mountains, called the Great Dividing Range, stretches down the eastern edge. It includes the highest point, Mount Kosciuszko, in the Snowy Mountains south of Canberra. Almost in the center of Australia is an isolated mountain of red sandstone rock that stands 1,142 feet (348 m) high and is about 5.8 miles (9.4 km) around at the base. It is called Uluru and is sacred to the Aboriginal people. It is one of Australia's greatest tourist attractions and has become a national symbol.

Facts at a Glance

Highest Point: Mount Kosciuszko 7,313 feet (2,229 m)

Longest River: Murray River 1,572 miles (2,530 km)

Coastline: 16,007 miles (25,760 km)

The Three Sisters rocks, in the Blue Mountains near Sydney, are visited by thousands of tourists and hikers every year.

DID YOU KNOW?

In February 2009, Australia suffered its worst bushfire ever. Known as "Black Saturday," the fires on February 7 killed 173 people and destroyed thousands of homes.

Mineral Wealth

Australia's rocks, some of which are 3.5 billion years old, bring great wealth to the country. They contain valuable minerals, including gold, diamonds, opals, copper, iron ore, coal, and uranium.

Water Shortages

Australia has few rivers. The water that these contain is in high demand from farmers, industries, and settlements. Water shortages are a major problem in Australia, especially in large urban centers. Water recycling and new farming methods are helping save water, while underground wells help meet demand. Education is also playing a part with programs that encourage saving water.

Warm and Dry

Australia is a generally warm and dry country. The center has the most extreme conditions, with very little rainfall and extremely high temperatures. The coastal regions of the east and south have a more pleasant climate, similar to southern Europe. This is where most agriculture is based. The northeast of Australia, around Cairns, has a tropical climate with rain forests and tropical wildlife, such as parrots and tree frogs.

▶ With an average rainfall of less than 2.4 inches (60 mm), Australia is the driest inhabited continent. Human demands on water mean that rivers and lakes, such as Lake Wivenhoe in Queensland, regularly dry out.

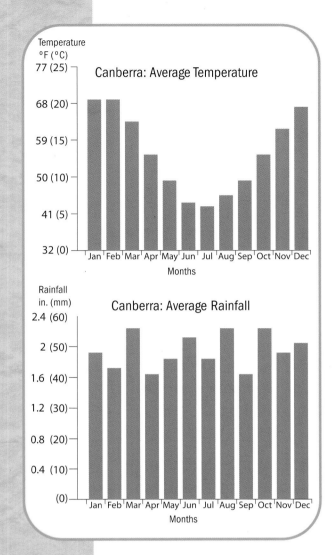

Temperature °F (°C)

Canberra: Average Temperature

Months

Rainfall in. (mm)

Canberra: Average Rainfall

Months

Population and Health

In 2010, Australia had a population of 21.5 million. The country's population grows by around 18,000 people each month. This puts pressure on the state to meet the needs of its growing population.

The Australian People

At the last population census in 2006, Australia had around 464,000 Aboriginal people, 33,000 Torres Strait Islanders, and about 20,000 people who were members of both groups. In total, Indigenous Australians made up about 2.5 percent of the country's population.

Most Australians today are descended from people who arrived from elsewhere in the world. The majority of these came from Europe, but immigrants also included people from Asia, the Middle East, Africa, and the Americas. Non-European immigrants have mainly arrived since the 1980s. This mixing of people from around the world has made Australia a very multicultural society. Sydney, for example, is famous for its Chinatown neighborhood

Members of Melbourne's Greek community wear traditional costumes as they celebrate Greece's independence day.

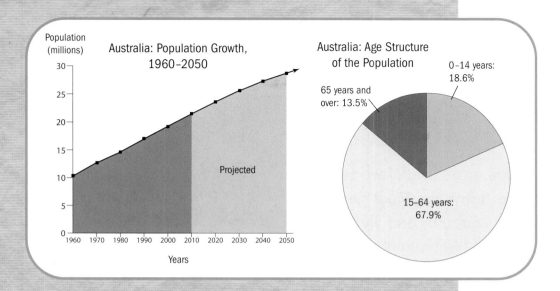

Australia: Population Growth, 1960–2050

Population (millions)

Projected

Years

Australia: Age Structure of the Population

0–14 years: 18.6%

65 years and over: 13.5%

15–64 years: 67.9%

and Melbourne has a large Greek community.

Health Matters

In general, Australian people take their personal health seriously. Most health issues are related to lifestyle choices (about diet, smoking, and drinking alcohol, for example) and to illnesses that are more common in aging populations, such as cancer and heart disease. Skin cancer is a particular problem in such a sunny climate. A national campaign called "Slip, Slop, Slap, Seek, Slide" is trying to educate people to protect themselves from the Sun better. It encourages people to slip on some clothing, slop on the sunscreen, slap on a hat, seek shelter when possible, and slide on some sunglasses.

⬤ These lifeguards on Bondi Beach, Sydney, are promoting Sun safety.

DID YOU KNOW?
Australia's Royal Flying Doctor Service sees around 270,000 patients per year, flying some 72,000 flights and travelling about 15 million miles (24 million km).

Settlements and Living

The vast central regions of Australia are too dry or hot to support large settlements. Most people live near the coast where it is cooler and wetter. In general, Australians enjoy high-quality housing and a good standard of living, similar to that of people in Europe or the USA.

An Urban Country

Around nine out of ten Australians live in an urban center, making Australia one of the most urbanized countries in the world. The largest cities are Sydney and Melbourne. Together with Brisbane, Perth, and Adelaide, they are home to 60 percent of all Australians. Rural settlements tend to be quite small and have normally developed because of mining or as centers for the farming industry.

Facts at a Glance

Urban Population:
90% (18.9 million)
Rural Population:
10% (2.4 million)
Population of Largest City:
4.4 million (Sydney)

🔻 There is no shortage of space in Australia. In the suburbs around the big cities, houses are often large and spread out, like these on the island of Tasmania.

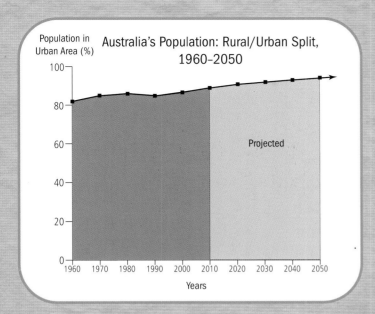

Population in Urban Area (%)

Australia's Population: Rural/Urban Split, 1960–2050

Projected

Years

Housing

Most city residents live in apartments or in houses. Wealthier neighborhoods often have large homes with gardens and swimming pools. Housing can be very expensive, so many people rent their homes rather than own them. Social housing from the government provides homes for the very poorest people. In rural areas, houses can be far from settlements or even from the nearest neighbor.

Social Divide

In general, Indigenous Australians have a lower standard of living than most Australians. For many years, the government neglected their needs. For example, their land was taken away and they had fewer services, such as health and education. Today, the government has made it illegal to treat Indigenous Australians differently and is supporting them in becoming a part of mainstream society. Indigenous Australians are now found among Australia's business and political leaders.

⬢ Samantha Harris is an internationally successful fashion model. She is also the first Aboriginal supermodel.

Family Life

Day-to-day family life in Australia is very similar to that in the USA. The trends are also similar, with climbing rates of divorce, people marrying later and having fewer children, and more people choosing to live on their own.

Mixed Marriages

Just over 30 percent of the marriages in Australia are between people who were born in different countries. Many of these are between people who come from the United Kingdom, Ireland, or New Zealand, but others include people from many other parts of the world, such as China, Vietnam, and the Philippines. This increase in mixed marriages is one sign of Australia becoming increasingly multicultural.

▼ Today, mixed marriages are increasingly common among Indigenous Australians. As a result of this, there are more mixed-race children.

Travelling Youth

Australia is a popular place for young travellers between the ages of 18 and 29. Many arrive and find temporary work in restaurants and shops, on farms, or in the tourist industry. They are an important part of the Australian economy in many places. The jobs they do are often available because young Australians also like to travel. Many Australians visit relatives overseas or go in search of better or higher-paid jobs. Others travel to study or simply to see parts of the world that are a long way from Australia.

Staying Connected

With around a quarter of the population born outside of Australia, connections with relatives who still live overseas are an important part of life for many families. These may involve visits abroad, or family members coming to Australia to visit. The Internet has made it easier and cheaper for families to stay in touch using e-mail or webcams, too.

◆ The grape harvest is a good opportunity for young people spending some time in Australia to find part-time work.

DID YOU KNOW?
Almost one in four Australians between the ages of 20 and 34 still lives with at least one parent. The high cost of housing and marrying later in life are two main causes of this trend.

Religion and Beliefs

Australians are free to follow whatever religion they choose. Close historical links with Europe mean that almost two-thirds of people follow Christianity, but this is lower than in the past as more recent settlers from other parts of the world have brought their various faiths with them.

Changes in Religion

Buddhism, Islam, and Hinduism are the other main religions followed by Australians and these are now growing much faster than Christianity. The number of Australians following Islam increased by about 70 percent between 1996 and 2006. In the same period, the number of people following Buddhism and Hinduism more than doubled.

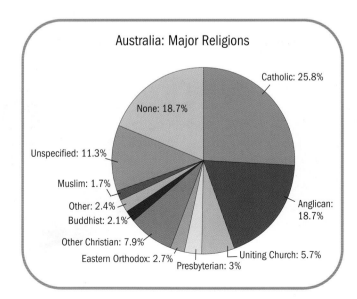

Australia: Major Religions

Catholic: 25.8%
None: 18.7%
Unspecified: 11.3%
Muslim: 1.7%
Other: 2.4%
Buddhist: 2.1%
Other Christian: 7.9%
Eastern Orthodox: 2.7%
Presbyterian: 3%
Uniting Church: 5.7%
Anglican: 18.7%

⬤ A Buddhist monk prays in a temple in Brisbane. The number of people following Buddhism in Australia has grown rapidly in recent decades, especially as more people arrive from Asia.

The increase in Islam, Hinduism, and Buddhism is leading to more mosques and temples being built in Australia, particularly in the major cities. Another major change relates to the number of Australians who say they have no religion. This had reached almost 19 percent of the population by 2006, up by more than a quarter since 1996.

Traditional Beliefs

Many Indigenous Australians have adopted Christianity, but traditional beliefs remain strong and some people follow both. For the Aboriginal people, the land is at the heart of their beliefs. Aboriginal beliefs or laws come from the Dreaming. This is a spoken story that tells how the spirits of their ancestors came to Earth and created the rocks, plants, animals, and other elements of the landscape. The ancestors then turned into the stars, trees, rocks, water holes, and other objects that Aborigines consider sacred today.

▼ A few sacred places have become known because they were under threat. The most famous of these is Uluru. This was also known as Ayers Rock before the Australian government returned it to the Aboriginal people in 1985.

Education and Learning

Australia has a good education system, from preschools to colleges and universities. The high standard of education has also made it attractive to students from Asia, many of whom come to study in Australia.

Schooling

Australia's system of schools is split into primary and secondary levels. All pupils must go to school between the ages of 6 and 15. They can then choose whether to stay on for one or two years. Around two-thirds of schools are state-funded, with the other third being mainly private Catholic schools, where parents pay for their children's schooling.

Facts at a Glance

Children in Primary School:
Male 96%, Female 97%
Children in Secondary School:
Male 87%, Female 88%
Literacy Rate (Over 15 Years):
99%

▼ Schoolchildren usually wear uniforms, which include dresses for girls and shirts and shorts for boys. Blazers are often worn by private-school pupils.

All pupils follow a national curriculum, with more choice in which subjects they study as they get older. The government promotes some subject areas to try to create the sorts of skills needed for the economy. These include languages, such as Chinese and Indonesian, computer skills, and science and technology.

Colleges and Universities

English-language colleges are common in Australia's larger cities and attract many students from Asia who want to learn English. These colleges are also popular with Asian businesspeople. Other colleges offer job-focused courses, such as catering, tourism, computer skills, or hairdressing. Australia has many universities. Sydney University is the oldest in the country and was opened in 1850.

Hard to Reach

Australia's vast size means that some remote communities are hard to reach, making educating the children who live there difficult. Some children live too far from school to travel there daily and so must board or have lessons at home by mail, Internet, and radio.

This isolation is one reason why Indigenous Australians, many of whom live in remote areas, have performed less well in school. In 2006, around 75 percent of 15–19 year olds were in school, but, for Indigenous Australians in the same age group, this fell to around 50 percent. This reduces the opportunities for Indigenous Australians to find jobs and improve their living conditions. If they do find work, it is often in lower-skilled and lower-paid jobs.

⚠ Australian universities are popular among foreign students, including those from Asia. In 2010, there were 593,000 overseas students in Australian universities.

DID YOU KNOW?
In 1948, a "school of the air" was started using radios to teach lessons to Outback children. Today, there are 16 schools of the air delivering lessons to children in remote areas.

Employment and Economy

Australia has one of the world's wealthiest economies. It has a major role in the world economy and was a founding member of the G20, a group of 20 leading economies from around the world.

A Modern Economy

Most of Australia's income comes from providing services, such as banking, insurance, tourism, telecommunications, and transportation. This sector also includes health and education services. Industry and manufacturing contribute around a quarter of all income, with mining being especially important. Agriculture provides just 4 percent of income, but includes some very important exports, such as grain, sheep, and wine.

Facts at a Glance

Contributions to GDP:
Agriculture: 4%
Industry: 26%
Services: 70%

Labor Force:
Agriculture: 4%
Industry: 21%
Services: 75%

Female Labor Force:
45% of total

Unemployment Rate:
5.6%

▼ Tourism provides many Australians with jobs guiding tourists, as these people are doing on Fraser Island. Many of these jobs are seasonal and do not provide employment for the whole year.

Employment

In July 2010, a little over 11.2 million people were employed in Australia, with most working in offices, stores, and public services. Modern machinery and technology has reduced the need for workers in manufacturing, industry, and agriculture. Some jobs are only available seasonably. For example, workers are taken on temporarily during the grape harvest.

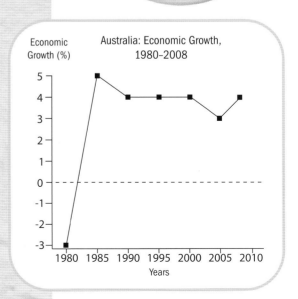

⬤ Restaurant staff form an important part of the service industry, especially in cities such as Sydney.

Global Economic Crisis

Australia survived the global economic crisis of 2008 better than most other countries. It continued to grow when many others went into recession. This was partly due to its location and strong trading relationships with Asia, a region of the world that continued to grow when economies in Europe and North America began to slow down. Unemployment increased slightly because of the recession, but this had already begun to recover by 2010.

DID YOU KNOW?
Over 2.5 million tourists have climbed over the top of Sydney Harbour Bridge to look down on the city 439 feet (134 m) below.

Indigenous Employment

The unemployment rate among Indigenous Australians is about three times higher than the national unemployment rate and continues to be a major challenge. Lower education levels and the remoteness of many indigenous communities (far from where there are jobs) are two of the main reasons for this. Government programs to help Indigenous Australians find employment have had mixed success and have often focused on low-skilled and part-time work.

Australia: Economic Growth, 1980–2008

Economic Growth (%)

Industry and Trade

Ever since the discovery of gold in Australia in 1851, mining and the processing of minerals has been one of the most important industries in Australia.

World Leader

Australia is a major mineral producer and exporter. It is the world's leading producer of bauxite, which is used to make aluminium. It is also a leading producer of gold, iron ore, nickel, uranium, titanium, zinc, diamonds, silver, coal, and copper. This mineral wealth is important for trade. Australia is the world's biggest exporter of coal, providing coal for power plants as far away as the United Kingdom.

Manufacturing

Machinery production and metal processing are two of the most important manufacturing industries in Australia. Food and drink manufacture and the processing of gasoline and chemical products are also major industries.

DID YOU KNOW?

Australian trains used to transport coal can have six locomotives and 148 cars. They can stretch to more than 1.25 miles (2 km) in length. A train that big can carry 9,370 tons (8,500 t) of coal.

▼ Coober Pedy is at the heart of Australia's opal mining industry. A series of small mines produces the world's best opals.

Altogether, manufacturing industries make up about ten percent of Australia's income, producing goods for export as well as local use.

Trade Links

Trade is important to the Australian economy and almost all of its trade in goods is transported by sea. Much of this trade is shipped in containers that come and go through massive ports, such as Port Botany, in Sydney. Australia's location means that most of its trade is with economies in Asia and particularly with China. Most of the country's exports are raw materials and agricultural goods. These go mainly to China, Japan, South Korea, and India. Australia's imports include machinery, equipment, and computers, which come mostly from China, the USA, Japan, and Thailand.

⏃ This ship is being loaded with coal in Newcastle, New South Wales. Coal is one of Australia's most important exports.

Australia: Major Export Partners

USA: 5%
UK: 4.4%
New Zealand: 4.1%
Other: 30.1%
South Korea: 7.9%
India: 7.5%
Japan: 19.2%
China: 21.8%

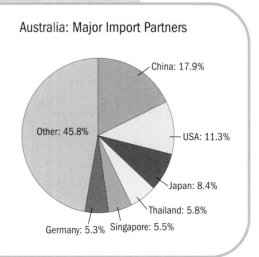

Australia: Major Import Partners

China: 17.9%
Other: 45.8%
USA: 11.3%
Japan: 8.4%
Thailand: 5.8%
Singapore: 5.5%
Germany: 5.3%

Farming and Food

Farming in Australia is limited by the climate and lack of water, but Australia is still a major food producer. Australians enjoy a truly global range of food, but traditional diets are under threat because of an increase in the consumption of fast food.

Grazers and Grain

More than half of the land in Australia is farmland. Most of the farms are used for grazing sheep or cattle, which are kept for meat, dairy products, and, in the case of sheep, wool. Australia produces about a quarter of the world's wool. Cereal crops, such as wheat and barley, take up most of the remaining farmland.

DID YOU KNOW?

In 2008, Australia had around 28 million cows and 77 million sheep. This was the equivalent of 1.3 cows and 3.6 sheep for every person.

▼ Livestock farming is important in Australia. Most sheep or cattle are kept on enormous ranches.

In Queensland and New South Wales, sugarcane is an important crop. Fruits (such as mangoes, bananas, oranges, apples, and tomatoes) and vegetables (including potatoes, carrots, onions, and mushrooms) are grown across Australia.

Australian Wine

Viticulture, or grape-growing, is an important industry in Australia. Most of the country's grapes are used to make wine. In 2010, Australia was the world's fourth-biggest wine exporter, with its wines sold in more than 100 countries worldwide.

A Global Feast

Australia's multicultural population is reflected in its food. Asian, European, and African flavors are found in all major cities and are even mixing to create new "fusion" dishes. Meat and fish play an important part in the diet and are often cooked outside on a barbecue, or "barbie" as it is known in Australia. However, fast food is on the increase and health officials are worried about growing levels of obesity linked to this.

⬤ Fishing is a significant industry in Australia and it has some of the largest and most modern fish markets in the world, such as this one in Sydney.

DID YOU KNOW?
There are around 2,000 wine companies in Australia, employing some 31,000 people and crushing nearly 2.2 million tons (2 million t) of grapes every year!

Transportation and Communications

The distances involved in travelling in Australia are enormous. The road journey from Sydney to Perth, for example, is about 2,450 miles (3,950 km) and driving non-stop would take about two days! This means that other forms of transportation and communication are vital to both people and businesses.

Air Travel

Sydney, Melbourne, Brisbane, and Perth are Australia's main international airports and between them account for nearly all the passengers who come and go from Australia each year. Domestic and regional air travel is just as important in Australia because of the large distances involved. Over half a million flights provide vital connections for some 50 million passengers each year, reducing the journey time between Sydney and Perth to between 4 and 5 hours.

⬤ The monorail in Sydney operates on a small loop in the city center. It connects with suburban train and bus services to allow people to travel further.

To help cover the large distances, Australia has enormous trucks and trailers, known as "Road Trains." These can be more than 164 feet (50 m) long.

Local Travel

At the local level, road and rail transportation are the most usual methods of travel. There are around 12 million cars registered in Australia, but, because of the huge distances involved, most car travel takes place locally within the state where the car is registered. Larger cities suffer from serious traffic problems, so many people use buses or urban railways as an alternative. Cities, such as Sydney, are trying to integrate public transportation by building new stations where people can easily swap from buses to trains.

Telephone and Internet

The number of households with an Internet connection increased by more than five times between 1998 and 2008. The Internet has had similar growth in the business and public sectors. In such a large country, the Internet has allowed businesses and services to reach remote communities more easily. Despite this, remote communities in the Outback, farming areas, and the island of Tasmania remain less connected than the rest of Australia. Cell phone use has grown even faster than the Internet and there are now more than twice as many cell phones as landline phones.

DID YOU KNOW?
The world's longest length of straight road is found on Australia's Nullabor Plain. It is 90 miles (146.6 km) long.

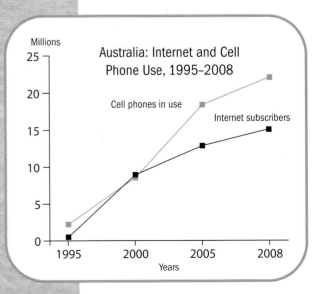

Australia: Internet and Cell Phone Use, 1995–2008

Millions

Cell phones in use

Internet subscribers

Years

Leisure and Tourism

Leisure in Australia is focused on sports and outdoor activities, socializing with friends and family, and enjoying cultural attractions.

Sports

Australians are among the world's best athletes in sports such as rugby, cricket, and tennis. They are also leaders in watersports including surfing, which plays a big part in Australia's beach culture. This love of sports was showcased when Sydney hosted the Olympic Games in 2000. Australians like to participate in sports, with walking, aerobic exercises, and swimming the most popular.

Sydney Opera House is one of the world's most famous buildings and Australia's top tourist attraction. It is also at the heart of the cultural activities in Sydney, with events throughout the year.

Cultural Attractions

Australians enjoy cultural activities and for many they are a regular part of their leisure time. Movies are the most widely enjoyed, followed by zoos and aquariums, libraries, and gardens. Art galleries, museums, theater performances, and music concerts are also popular. Major cultural events include Chinese New Year and Mardi Gras, and there are hundreds of local and national arts and music festivals. Aboriginal art and music is popular in Australia, and Aboriginal artworks are among the best-selling tourist souvenirs.

World-Famous Australians

Australia has produced many stars. Rugby player David Campese and Formula One racer Mark Webber are among Australia's famous sports stars. Famous Indigenous Australian sportswomen include the tennis player Evonne Goolagong Cawley and the runner Cathy Freeman. Kylie Minogue is one of Australia's best-known pop stars and its movie stars include Cate Blanchett, Nicole Kidman, and Hugh Jackman.

Tourists

Australia is a popular tourist destination, with most tourists coming from New Zealand, the United Kingdom, Japan, the USA, and China. Most visitors arrive in Sydney, and the Opera House, Sydney Harbour Bridge, and the nearby Blue Mountains are some of the city's top attractions. Other popular places to visit include the Great Barrier Reef, Uluru, Kakadu National Park, the vineyards, and major cities including Melbourne, Perth, and Brisbane.

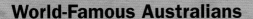 Hundreds of people flock to Australia's beautiful beaches, especially on holidays such as Boxing Day, on December 26.

Facts at a Glance

Tourist Arrivals (Millions)

Year	Arrivals
1995	3.7
2000	4.9
2005	5.5
2008	5.6

Environment and Wildlife

Australia's physical separation from the rest of the world has led to the development of some unique wildlife and environments. These are a major tourist attraction, but many are also under threat, so tourism must be carefully balanced with conservation.

Only in Australia

Australia's unique wildlife includes the kangaroo, wombat, emu, platypus, and koala, but these are just a few of its nearly 17,000 species. This biodiversity is most obvious at the Great Barrier Reef, off the northeast coast. The reef is made up of millions of creatures called corals, making it the world's largest living thing. Each year, about 2 million people visit it. Tourism needs to be carefully monitored to avoid damage to the reef. The reef is one of many protected areas in Australia that include more than 500 national parks.

Facts at a Glance

Proportion of Area Protected:
6.7%

Biodiversity (Known Species):
16,865

Threatened Species: 179

⬥ The koala is one of the most recognizable Australian animals. Like kangaroos, koalas are marsupials, or mammals that carry their young in pouches.

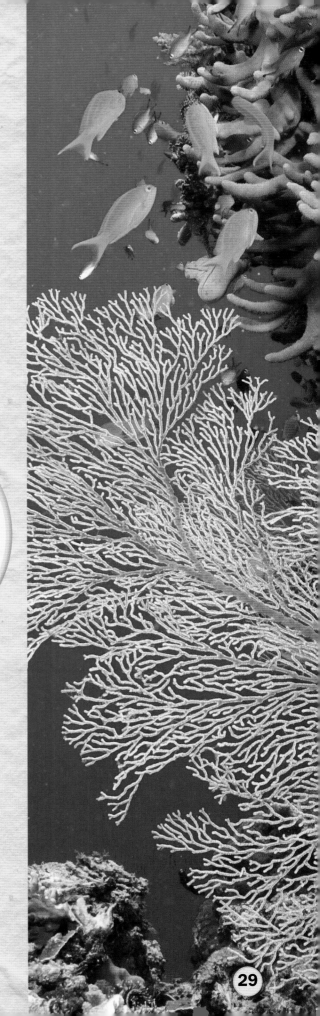

Climate Change and Water

One of the biggest threats to the Great Barrier Reef is global warming. Climate change, caused in part by pollution from human activities, is warming Earth's oceans. As the seas warm, some species of coral are dying because of the higher water temperature. Climate change is also worsening the problem of water shortages in Australia. This leads to more droughts and the drying up lakes and rivers. Australia is investing in renewable energy, building improvements, recycling, and education programs to try to reduce its own contributions to climate change.

Foreign Pests

A serious threat to Australia's wildlife and environments comes from overseas pests. These are known as invasive species because they tend to take over areas and push out local plants and animals. They include plants, such as alligator weed and blackberries, and animals, such as rabbits and the cane toad. The government helps to fund efforts to reduce the spread of invasive species and there are now strict checks at airports and ports to prevent other invasive species from arriving in Australia.

DID YOU KNOW?
Between 1901 and 1907, the government of Western Australia built a fence to try to stop the spread of rabbits, an invasive species that destroyed crops. The fence failed and rabbits are still a pest.

▶ The Great Barrier Reef stretches a total distance of 1,250 miles (2,000 km) and is home to more than 1,500 species of fish. It is the largest reef in the world, but is under threat from a warming climate and large numbers of tourists.

Glossary

aerobic exercises (er-OH-bik EK-ser-sy-zez) Activities that are good for breathing and blood circulation.

bauxite (BOK-syt) A clay-like substance that is the main source of aluminum.

biodiversity (by-oh-dih-VER-sih-tee) The number of different types of living things that are found in a certain place on Earth.

board (BORD) To stay at the school one is attending.

cancer (KAN-ser) A sickness in which cells multiply out of control and do not work properly.

census (SEN-sus) An official count of people in various places.

climate change (KLY-mut CHAYNJ) Changes in Earth's weather that were caused by things people did.

Commonwealth of Nations (KAH-mun-welth UV NAY-shunz) A group of countries that were once ruled by the United Kingdom.

conservation (kon-sur-VAY-shun) Protecting something from harm.

continent (KON-tuh-nent) One of Earth's seven large landmasses.

culture (KUL-chur) The beliefs, practices, and arts of a group of people.

divorce (dih-VORS) The legal ending of a marriage.

export (ek-SPORT) A good or service that is sold to another country.

global warming (GLOH-bul WAWRM-ing) A gradual increase in how hot Earth is. It is caused by gases that are released when people burn fuels such as gasoline.

immigrants (IH-muh-grunts) People who move to a new country from another country.

import (IM-port) A good brought from one country to another.

indigenous (in-DIH-jeh-nus) Having started in and coming naturally from a certain area.

invasive species (in-VAY-suv SPEE-sheez) Animals or plants that were brought to a place and threaten the animals and plants that naturally live there.

mineral (MIN-rul) Natural matter that is not an animal, a plant, or another living thing.

mosque (MOSK) A place of worship and prayer for Muslims.

multicultural (mul-tee-KULCH-rul) Composed of different groups of people.

recession (rih-SEH-shun) A time when many businesses close and people are laid off.

road train (ROHD TRAYN) A truck with several parts that is used to cary goods long distances.

sacred (SAY-kred) Holy.

service sector (SIR-vis SEK-tor) The part of an economy made up of services, such as education or healthcare.

temple (TEM-pel) A place where people go to worship.

urbanized (UR-buh-nyzd) Having lots of people living in cities.

viticulture (VIH-ti-kul-cher) The growing of grapes, mostly for making wine.

Topic Web

Use this topic web to explore Australian themes
in different areas of study.

Math
Find out how many Australian dollars there are in 1 US dollar. Now work out how much some everyday items (for example, a bottle of water, an apple, a bus ticket) would cost you in Australian dollars.

Citizenship
Indigenous Australians have been treated unfairly in the past, but there are laws now to avoid this inequality. What do we mean by "inequality?" Use a spider diagram to explore your understanding of this word.

English
Think of three questions you have about living in Australia after reading this book. Write a letter to a young person in Australia asking for the answers to your questions.

Science
Australia has many important minerals, including coal. Find out how coal is formed and how it is mined. Why is coal a non-renewable resource?

Australia

Information Technology
Imagine that you are planning a vacation in Australia. Use the Internet to find out when the best time to go is and what the main things to visit would be.

Design and Technology
Sydney Opera House has a famous design based on the sails of a ship. Think of an object to inspire your imagination and design a building based on this.

Geography
Australia is the world's largest island. Find out what the next three largest islands in the world are. How do they compare to Australia in size and population? Where are they located?

History
Find out what you can about the Aboriginal people of Australia. How were they treated unfairly by the Europeans who arrived to settle in Australia?

Further Reading, Web Sites, and Index

Further Reading

Australia by Colleen Sexton (Bellwether Media, 2010)
Endangered Animals of Australia by Marie Allgor (PowerKids Press, 2011)
Focus on Australia by Otto James (Gareth Stevens, 2007)

Web Sites

Due to the changing nature of Internet links, PowerKids Press has developed an online list of Web sites related to the subject of this book. This site is updated regularly. Please use this link to access the list: www.powerkidslinks.com/discovc/aus/

Index